# Old Insch

## Ann Dean

Insch from Denwell Road, with corn 'stooks' waiting to be gathered in. On the left is the chimney of the gas works which served the village from 1830 until 1936. Coal for the gas works was brought to Insch by train after 1854; before then it had to be brought 14 miles by horse and cart from the canal terminus at Port Elphinstone. The long terraced building in the centre is the 'Timmer Terrace', still standing, off Market Street, down a lane once called Dubbystile. On the right the double cottage was the 'Peer's Hoose', one end for the women with a resident caretaker and the other end for the men. Insch's poor house was erected in 1853, administered by the parochial board and financed by the poor rates. The local doctor looked after the poor house residents and also attended and gave parish financial support to those sick and elderly poor who were still able to live at home.

Text © Ann Dean, 2012.
First published in the United Kingdom, 2012,
by Stenlake Publishing Ltd.
Telephone: 01290 551122
www.stenlake.co.uk

ISBN 9781840335989

## Acknowledgements

I wish to thank the trustees and the volunteers of Insch Connection Museum for their help in choosing some of the photographs for this book and for all the information they made available to me. Also I thank Aberdeen Journals for the use of two of their photographs (pages 2 and 5). As always, I have to acknowledge the help of the local studies department at Aberdeenshire Libraries, Oldmeldrum.

## Bibliography

Clemo, Margaret Garson, *Historic Insch*, 3rd & Updated Ed., 2009
Davidson, Rev. John, *Inverurie and the Earldom of the Garioch*, Edinburgh, 1878
Shepherd, Ian, *Gordon, An Illustrated Architectural Guide*, 1994
Sinclair, Sir John, ed., *The Statistical Account of Scotland*, Vol.xvii, 1790-99
*The New Statistical Account of Scotland*, Vol.xii, 1845
Smith, Alexander, ed., *A New History of Aberdeenshire*, 2 vols. Aberdeen, 1875

*Left*: Until 1936, the lighting of Insch's streets depended on gas lamps. W. R. Dressel, plumber and gas maintenance man cleaned and maintained the street lamps, each morning setting off to carry out maintenance work. At 5pm he was off again to light the lamps and at 10.30pm to extinguish them. There was no street lighting in the mornings and none all summer. On foot he was unmistakable, always wearing 'drill sheen' (gym shoes) and in his car, a yellow Citroen coupé, was equally conspicuous. Butchart's corner was the favourite meeting place for the older men folk of the village – a perfect spot for seeing all that was going on.

# Introduction

Insch lies at the heart of the Garioch, an area once known as 'the meal girnel' of Aberdeenshire. The name 'Insch' may derive from the Gaelic word signifying an island, a meadow or haugh with the early village beside the Shevock Burn. It is sheltered by the hills around it: Bennachie, Carriers' Hill, Hill of Christ's Kirk, Hill of Dunnydeer and the Foudland Hills. The Shevock Burn forms the parish boundary on the west and south. The many standing stones around Insch indicate that the area was inhabited from very early times. St. Drostan's Church, erected in the 1200s, is probably on the site of a much earlier St. Drostan's, founded by St. Drostan or one of his followers.

Insch was the 'Kirktoun' of the parish, with its church and manse, small school, market place and a few merchants, smiths, blacksmiths and miller. The Leith Hays of Leithhall possessed the lands of Insch and the superiority of the burgh and the feuars (people who owned their own houses) rented from Leithhall strips of land beyond the village. These strips they again let out to their tenants to cultivate and provide food for both feuars and tenants.

Changes in agriculture from the late 1700s altered the appearance of the countryside. The many small fermtouns throughout the parish gradually disappeared to be replaced by fewer, larger farms. More people left the land to settle in the village and went to farms as day labourers. The skills which had been in each fermtoun were now to be found in the village: the weavers, tailors and dressmakers, bakers, shoemakers, wrights, blacksmiths and saddlers. The increase in population meant more house building and the village spread from its small nucleus around the kirk and market. Wealthier merchants built more impressive houses and then when the railway arrived in 1854, Insch changed dramatically. The population increased again, banks appeared, as did hotels, a post office and a postal delivery service, chemists – everything considered necessary for a flourishing village.

Dr. George Currie, aware that poor water from village wells and no proper sewage disposal were the cause of many infections and epidemics, finally achieved his desired objective in the 1890s, – a supply of fresh running water available to every household and a proper sewage disposal system.

The railway had a narrow escape from Dr. Beeching's proposed cuts, and today Insch has a more frequent rail service than at any time in the past. Although the shops have dwindled in number, the population and housing have increased greatly. So many people have discovered the advantages of living in a village with all its amenities and yet being able to work in the larger towns and the city of Aberdeen, making full use of the railway to do so.

*This page and opposite*: Enterprising businessman, James Souter, with his brother John came to Insch in 1901 from the village of Rhynie which was 10 miles from the nearest railway station. On the death of his brother, John, a timber man, took over the business, developed the sawmill and expanded into the building trade. His family followed him in the business. The shop became a magnet for not only the people of the village but also the farming community and folk from Aberdeen and all over the north-east, with bee-keepers in particular depending on Souter's for all their equipment. The firm produced electricity at its sawmill from 1913 to 1936 for 100 houses and from 1922 for the hospital. After that Grampian Electricity Supply Company supplied the village with electricity.

The staff of the general merchant's shop gathers outside on the High Street in 1894. John Russell is wearing a hat with his son George to his left, holding his eldest daughter, Jean. John was an apprentice in Bisset's general store across High Street, and saw the potential in business with the coming of the railway in 1854, starting up his own shop in 1856.

George Russell introduced tailoring and dressmaking and about 1910, a tweed department. He travelled all over Scotland selecting the finest tweeds and knitwear. Mr. William Lippe shows a potential customer a length of tweed from well-stocked shelves.

Queen Elizabeth, The Queen Mother and Princess Margaret made several visits to Russell's, from about 1950 and enjoyed afternoon tea with the Russell family.

*Opposite*: This group of tailors indicate how much work and employment the Tweed Room gave to local men: from the left – William Jamieson, John Geddes, Peter Beattie, Jock McRobbie, unknown standing on the left, George or John Tait, the cutter, standing on the right, Jack Glennie, Sandy Robertson, Jimmy Duffus, Bob Bandeen, unknown and Jimmy Durno.

Beechcroft Terrace was named after the Beech Croft, owned by the Russells. Beyond the terrace were the fields cultivated by them, where they kept their milking cow and the pony for delivering goods and its shed. The cow was milked in a byre in Martin Lane, at the back of Russell's shop.

In the early 1900s the name 'Backtoun' was still used instead of 'Martin Lane' despite having been renamed in 1892 after the popular Provost Martin. It was opposite this row of cottages that the Russell's cow went in and out of her byre followed by an old farm hand.

Willam Johnstone, from a long line of blacksmiths in the Largie area, moved to Insch over 100 years ago and settled at the smiddy in Dunnydeer Road. In the early days over 700 horses were on the smiddy books, with three anvils in constant use and two assistant blacksmiths to help tackle the volume of work.

Alexander followed his father William, with his son Adam working with him. Adam's son, also Adam, became the smiddy's last Johnstone blacksmith. In front of the smiddy the blacksmiths line up, the two assistants, Adam and his father Alexander.

The Dunnydeer Road (one of the district's oldest roads) to Huntly passes the smiddy, the second building on the right, then through the trees ('The Belts'). On the right hand side of the road there is still a section of old paling.

*Opposite*: Helen Boyd's cottage, next door to the smiddy, was also called 'The Belts' and named after the plantation of trees further up the road. In this photograph Helen Boyd, on the left, is relaxing in her Orkney chair, wearing her tartan skirt, made at Russells and her mother on the right is reading.

The general merchant's shop in The Square, 'Cooper and Harper's', was established in 1905 by Allan Cooper and Lewis Harper. The business was run by both men until the death of Cooper in 1919 and since then solely by members of the Harper family but the shop has never lost its double name. Next door to it, later incorporated into the shop, was Insch Post Office. This photograph was taken around 1914. It was the post office's second move since its beginnings when mail arrived off the mail coach at Old Rayne and any letters for Insch were brought by runner and left at the shop which later became known as 'Butchart's shop'. In 1854 when the mail came directly to Insch on the mail train, Insch became the main post office for the area and the post office moved to its second home, a building on the other side of the High Street, almost opposite its third premises beside Cooper and Harper's.

In 1925 the post office moved to premises on Commerce Street where it has remained. At the time of this photograph, the post office was in the hands of James A. Reid. He and his son C. A. Reid were postmasters from 1924 to 1970. Next to the post office is the Commercial Hotel.

Insch is at the heart of the Garioch, a rich agricultural district. Ploughing matches were and still are very popular among the farming community. Up to the mid-1900s, the ploughman had to show that he could handle a team of horses as well as plough a good furrow.

This photograph was taken at Dunnydeer Farm, with George Munro fourth from the left. The harvest corn was cut by a team of men wielding their scythes.

Willie Reid was a well-known thresher and haulage contractor in the district; it was his 'stem mull' and workers that farms depended on to thrash their corn. In this photograph circa 1900 Dunnydeer Hill is in the background. The packs of thrashed corn, would have been on their way to the mill at Insch.

There have been several mills around Insch, powered by the Shevock Burn; early records point to one at Mill of Rothney and the other at the Drumrossie end of the village. In the late 1850s both mills ceased working and the mill at the centre of the village was built, a much more impressive affair with water diverted from the Shevock along a lade to drive the water wheel. A husk mill nearby was built to produce animal feed from the husks; it had a tall red brick chimney belching out steam, so locally was called the 'stem stack'.

MARKET DAY AT INSCH.

B.8587

The mart was built in 1898. Previously, markets were held in The Square or on Market Green, but with the coming of the railway, and improvements in farming and the large increase in livestock production, the mart was badly needed. Cattle and sheep could be loaded on to rail trucks at the nearby railway sidings to travel to markets in the south. Market day (seen here in 1950) was always Monday, when farmers and their wives came to the village.

DUNNYDEER ROAD, INSCH. 93534 J.V.

On the relatively traffic free roads up to the 1950s, cattle and sheep were frequently driven along main and side roads to and from the market. Here a flock is being shepherded from the market, up 'The Belts', perhaps to Dunnydeer Farm.

22

St. Sair's Fair was held annually in early July in a field between Insch and the village of Colpy. It was principally a horse fair, but like all fairs there were many attractions for everyone. After the sale the horses and ponies were taken to Insch Station, but on reaching Insch they had their shoes removed lest in kicking they damaged other horses or the railway trucks. Farm workers would earn an extra shilling to ride a horse, or lead a string of them to the smiddy in Western Road, opposite the church. At the end of a fair day, there was a large pile of horse shoes on the smiddy floor.

THE INSTITUTE, INSCH.

213255.J.V.

The Institute was opened in 1929, erected and endowed in memory of John Russell, merchant in Insch for 50 years by his son Dr. John Russell, O.B.E. Dr. Russell also gave the bowling green and his library to the village. The building originally contained the library, the town council's meeting room, a billiard room and the offices of the bowling club. It is seen here in 1931.

The bowling club was formed in 1930 and is still very popular. Lying between the Institute and the Shevock Burn, it enjoys a view of Bennachie to the south and Dunnydeer Hill to the west. In 2011 an impressive complex was added to the existing Institute.

The tennis club was formed in 1922 on land donated by the Leith-Hays of Leithhall. The hard courts were better suited to the low-lying position near the Shevock Burn than the grass court, which had been previously and unsuccessfully tried in 1896 next to the curling pond. Tennis was very popular with young people in the village, with participation in various tennis leagues. In 1986 the courts were superceded by all-weather courts at the Bennachie Leisure Centre.

*Right*: Insch had two main hotels, the Commercial Hotel and the Station Hotel and from time to time there were other smaller establishments, such as the Temperance Hotel where this menu would certainly not have appeared. It is a joy to read, even though a good Scots Dictionary might have to be dipped into; knowledge of local places can help too.

*Above*: In the 1940s and 50s there was a flourishing Strathspey and Reel Society. Its concerts were conducted by the station master, Mr. W. Cruickshank. Mr. J. Murray, then chemist, was one of the fiddlers and a composer. In the back row of the group are George Dickie, Sandy Robertson, Netherton, Jack Petrie, and the pianist Mary Minty; in the front row are Frank Anderson, John Dickie, Lediken, J. Murray, Alan Davidson, Ardoyne, Donald Shand, Oyne and their conductor, William Cruickshank.

# INSCH MENU.

Cocky Leeky ; Sheep's Heid Broth ; Farls o' Cakes ;
Mornin' Mist aff Foudland.

Saumon' gaffed frae the Ury ; Shevock Halibut, Herrin'
an' Yallow Haddocks ; Caller Ou Sauce.
A Drappie o' Jericho.

The Haggis, Great Chieftain o' the Puddin' Race.
Mountain Dew fae Benachie.

The Biled Jigot o' a Blackfaced Wether ; Saut Beef an'
Curly Kale fae Culsalmond ; Chappit Taties ; Biled Neeps
an' Carrots ; Bubbly Jock wi' Cranberry Sauce ; Stot's
Ribs Roasted ; Green Pizz ; Sheep's Heid an' Trotters
(Singt at Robin Tamson's Smiddy) ; The Hin' Leg o'
Jock Samson's Soo ; Birsled Taties ; Tammy's Taes ;
Venison Pasty ; Wild Dueks ; Peesweeps ; Whawps ;
Pertricks, an' Muir Fools aff Benachie.
A Moofu' o' Teacher's Ardmore Highland Cream
fae Kennethmont

Bramble Tairts ; Epple Tairts ; Ploom Tairts ; Trimlin'
Tam ; Rouly Pouley ; Rothney Marmalade ; Kebbucks
an' Crowdie fae Auchleven ; Shortbreid ; Cookies ;
Sweeties, an' Plunky.

Toddy made wi' Dooty Free Fusky.
A Cup o' Tay wi' a Cinder In't.
Oyne Wine an' Sneeshin.
Deoch an' Dorus.

*from Jessie*

27

*Below*: 'The Clooses' (*clooses* is Scots for 'sluice') – the local name for the pool formed by the shut sluice gate – was a fine but small swimming pool and a great place for children to 'dook' in the summer.

*Opposite*: Gala day in Insch was held annually usually towards the end of June. This photograph dates from the late 1940s, with Provost J. Riddoch on the left. So many faces are recognisable in the crowd: ex-Provost C. Beattie, Mrs. Melvin, Red Cross assistant, and Mr. George Munro who is featured in a previous photo scything at Dunnideer when younger. By the dress of the children it can be seen that competitive sport was very important, possibly more so than the refreshments and entertainments in the tent.

Only the gable end of old St. Drostan's Church survives, capped by a very fine carved bellcote. The photograph shows the bell in position, but it was subsequently taken down as unsafe. It was then lost and many years later found again and has come home to Insch, kept safe at the Insch Connection Museum. The graveyard is the haunt of those seeking their family histories. The building to the right was the Congregational Church, now the Freemason's Lodge. In the 1700s, a stone coffin slab, 6 feet by 20 inches, was unearthed in the graveyard, with the inscription *Orate pro anima raddfi sacerdotis* (pray for the soul of Radulf the priest): this slab would have covered the grave of Radulph, a chaplain to the bishop of Aberdeen from 1172 to 1199. It has been erected against the gable wall of the church.

The Parish Church in Western Road was built in 1883. The ceremony taking place in the photograph is the church parade on the day of King Edward VII's funeral in 1910. The piper may have been J. Mitchell, the drummer N. Fraser, followed by the town council, the 'Terriers' (the Territorials) and the public.

An early 1900s photograph of the church and Western Road shows Insch after a blizzard. It was a case then of everyone digging.

EPISCOPAL CHURCH AND RECTORY, INSCH

St. Drostan's Episcopal Church and Rectory were erected in 1894; the stone used was red granite. There was a mission in the Drill Hall from 1880, then in the Public Hall from 1899 until the church was built, during the incumbency of Rev. William Dodd. One well-known rector from 1938 to 1961 was Rev. Hardie Duthie, a fine musician and harpist. He was knowledgeable about fine paintings, antique furniture and objets d'art, particularly any which could adorn his private chapel in the rectory.

The hospital in Insch is known officially as 'Insch and District War Memorial Hospital' and is cherished by all local people. A 1922 newspaper cutting states the purpose of the hospital: 'To perpetuate the memory of men from their districts who fell in the war, the people of Insch and the neighbouring parishes of Premnay, Leslie, Culsalmond, Oyne and Chapel of Garioch have erected a handsome and splendidly equipped memorial hospital'. In the entrance hall of the hospital, there is a board on which are the names of people with Insch connections from all over the world, who gave donations and left legacies; here also are the memorial boards with the names of all the fallen of the district from both world wars.

Insch War Memorial Hospital had only two matrons between 1922 and 1973, Miss Scatterty (later Mrs. Beattie) from 1922 to 1939 and Miss Cruickshank from 1939 to 1973.

Dr. Mitchell was the general practitioner for Insch and district from 1909 to his death in 1952. He was immensely proud of the War Memorial Hospital, which was his responsibility, as both doctor and surgeon, from 1922 until his death. He worked tirelessly for the good of all his patients scattered throughout a very large practice.

Drumrossie House, on the outskirts of the village, has its roots in the 13th century. The present house is mainly an 1840s rebuilding of an older house. The estate of Drumrossie was made up of the lands of Drumrossie on the left bank of the Shevock and the lands of Rothney on the right. Owned mainly through the centuries by Gordons, the last owner of both Drumrossie and Rothney was a Leslie of Warthill. The estate was finally broken up in the 1920s with Drumrossie House left with policies of mature trees and the 'park' stretching from the house down to the Shevock. This was called the 'Show Park' as local agricultural shows and picnics were held there. In the Second World War, the area was used for the resting of Army battalions between their tours of active service.

During the First World War, Drumrossie House became a Red Cross Hospital for the nursing and recuperation of officers.

This view of the High Street, with Russell's shop on the immediate left, shows clearly the width of the street, indicating the market place of former times. Right in the middle of the picture is Insch's finest building, 'The Neuk', sadly demolished in the 1950s. Built in 1693 for the merchant and burgess of the burgh, William Logie, it was a very impressive house but lost to the village before the days of appreciating the value of retaining and restoring old buildings. In this Edwardian photo there is no sign of cars but ample evidence of horses, two fine new banks on the right, the Town and County Bank (now Lloyds TSB) and the North of Scotland Bank, later the Clydesdale Bank, the post office, and finally the house of Dr. Currie, a good doctor and local historian.

The High Street, looking from the other direction. The gas lamp was a popular gathering place for village discussions. The shop of Wilson the chemist on the corner is still, over 100 years later, bearing the same name and selling more or less the same goods. In the distance is the gable end of old St. Drostan's Church and a glimpse of Bennachie.

Once past old St. Drostan's Church, the other end of the High Street is in sight, ending at the bridge over the Shevrock Burn. Known officially as the Shevock Bridge, its local name for many years was 'McCracken's Briggie', named after the doctor who built his house and surgery in the 1860s, near the bridge on the right; he called it 'Emerald Bank'. In this photo, the house is just hidden by the immediate building, but one of 'Emerald Bank's' chimney stacks can be seen. At the side of the road (no pavement) there is a public water pump, which would indicate a photograph of the 1890s; in the village of Insch eleven water pumps were provided and beyond the Shevock Burn in Rothney, four.

Looking back from the Shevock Bridge up the High Street, the house on the right was built in the 1870s as the Congregational Church manse. 'Emerald Bank' is just visible amongst the trees. This end of the village appears to have lacked gas lighting.

Among the many shops lining this end of Commerce Street were a saddler, a bicycle repair shop, a baker, a shoe shop, a watchmaker and jeweller's and another shoe shop. Visible in the very centre of the photograph, where Western Road branches off to the right, is Alvah Cottage, Insch's first police station or as it was locally named 'the jile'.

COMMERCE St, INSCH

The middle section of Commerce Street, shows the railings on the left of the Public Hall built in 1869. Beyond the Public Hall, now known as the Community Centre, is Fordyce Hall, once a baker's shop, then the meeting place of the Christian Brethren. On the right, beyond Alvah Cottage's dyke, is the wall of the parochial school playground.

Commerce Street, Insch

Still on Commerce Street, this time looking towards The Square with J. Selbie at the door of his sweetie shop. There was no tarmac on the roads and a pavement only on one side of the street so it was 'affa stewie' in summer and 'affa dubby' in winter. Opposite the shop was a block of flats called 'West End'; at the back of the block were stone stairs leading to upper flats.

Beyond the sweetie shop on Commerce Street was Insch's second police station, with policeman George Christie on duty in 1901.

*Below*: The area around Insch and throughout the Garioch is rich in prehistoric monuments. The stones at Stonehead, about a half mile beyond Dunnydeer Hill, are all that is left of a stone circle probably erected around 4,000 years ago.

*Right*: The Picardy Stone, Largie, between Insch and the Foudland Hill, is a handsome example of Pictish art. Erected possibly as a memorial stone, the carvings may show rank or membership of a specific tribe. It dates from the 6th to 7th centuries A.D.

Dunnydeer Castle Insch.

M. 150.

Dunnydeer Castle, situated on the top of the Hill of Dunnydeer, is a prominent landmark. Over 2,000 years ago, there was a well-established oblong fort on the summit of the hill, still to be traced by the remaining sections of vitrified wall. Lower down the hill are later defensive earthwork ramparts. On the lower flanks of the hill, are signs of hut platforms. Finally on top of the deserted fort, in the 1200s a stone tower was built. All that now remains is the west wall with its fine pointed window and various smaller sections which indicate the shape of the tower.

Insch was created a Burgh of Barony by Mary Queen of Scots in 1565. Her Baron, Andrew Leslie, and his heirs and successors, had the duty each year, to choose bailies and officers in the burgh of Insch to be responsible for maintaining good order and enacting any rules and regulations for the good of the people. The burgh was granted permission to hold two free fairs, one on 'the day of St. James', 24th July (eventually to become St. Sair's Fair) and the other on the 14th December, St. Drostan's Day.

*Above*: This view of Insch, from Carrier's Hill, can be dated to about 1900. Insch Higher Grade School, erected in 1899, appears to be very much newly-built, sitting on its own surrounded by fields. The village has the shape of a horse-shoe, with the mill and all its extensions appearing to link the 'village' of Rothney to that of Insch, on the far side of the Shevock Burn. The husk mill's 'stem stack' stands out, opposite the mill. The parish church's hall, built in 1901 is not yet visible. At the station, the footbridge is between the station building and the signal box, its original position.

INSCH FROM SOUTH.                                                                           213253.

A 1931 view from Carrier's Hill shows how, within thirty years, Insch had grown and filled in, the horse-shoe shape gone. The Institute and bowling green are there and next to them, the War Memorial Hospital. Western Road and Charles Street are spreading towards Dunnydeer. At the station, the footbridge has been moved to its present position, on the other side of the station building. In this photograph, straight down Commercial Road to the bend in the road, there is Clifton, a large house demolished in the 1950s.

Rannes Terrace is a reminder that before the building of the hospital in 1922 and the Institute in 1929, there were no buildings beyond this group in the photograph. In the earlier 1900 'bird's eye' view, it shows the building on the right as the only one in the terrace, the next two built later with probably 'Greenhaugh' on the other side of the terrace already there.

Insch Station.

This is one of the earliest known photographs of Insch Station with the staff on the south platform. The footbridge in its original position masks the signal box beyond it. The level crossing gates are clearly seen and beside the gates on the north platform the water tower fed through a pipe from the Shevock Burn. Each day the entrance to the pipe was checked by a surfaceman from Wardhouse on his daily walk of inspection down the line to Insch Statiom.

This later view of the station shows clearly the north platform waiting room, the water crane at the end of the platform, and the re-positioned footbridge, using old rails dating from the late 1870s. The north platform wooden waiting room was built by the Great North of Scotland Railway to a standard pattern. Of the many throughout the north-east of Scotland, this is the sole survivor. Beyond the bridge is the large goods shed and beyond that are the sheds and stores close to the railway sidings, mainly for the bringing in of heavy goods into the village.

*Inset*: The Cycling Club Emblem on the wall of the Station Hotel.

The fountain was erected in 1893, with a drinking trough for horses. On the left is the Station Hotel built in the 1850s, originally known as Rothney Inn and from 1880 as the Station Hotel. It was the official venue of the Cyclists' Touring Club; their handsome logo can be seen on the front of the hotel. Cyclists travelled to Insch by train with their bicycles, lunched at the Station Hotel, completed their planned cycling trip and came back to the hotel for more refreshments before returning to Aberdeen by train. Between the fountain and the station fence, there was an army block-house during the Second World War, removed in 1946.

Mr. Scott's shop was on Commerce Street, behind the saddler's shop. The activities of the Cycling Club may have given him more business.

Commercial Road, Rothney, Insch is the title of this postcard view. At one time Insch and Rothney were two separate 'villages' in different parishes, the dividing line between them being the Shevock Burn, Rothney in Premnay and Insch in Insch Parish. Before 1854, Rothney was an estate with several small farms and crofts owned by Leslie of Warthill and Drumrossie but when the railway came in 1854, Rothney village grew from a cluster of buildings around the station to two streets of houses and shops, Gordon Terrace and Commercial Road. Eventually Rothney's Commercial Road and Insch's Commerce Street met. Rothney had its own town council until 1923 when it combined with Insch. On Commercial Road there were general merchants' shops, baker, newsagent, shoe shop, tailor – almost everything a village needed; only for the post office and the chemist did Rothney have to make a trip 'o'er the water' to Insch.

The Free Church School pupils and the pupils from the parochial school nearby (once Simpson's Garage and now the Co-operative) joined up at playtime. Some children wore boots and others were barefoot.

Public Schools, Insch.

Farquhar, Insch

This was built in 1899 and accommodated all the children from the parochial school, the Free Church School and the children from Rothney. The road linking the school to both the High Street and Rannes Street was named Alexander Street after one of the Leith Hay lairds.